The Victorian House

THE Victorian House

Robin Langley Sommer

With photographs by

Charles J. Ziga

CHARTWELL BOOKS, INC.

Above: *An eclectic Victorian with classical symmetry—Glen Auburn, in Natchez, Mississippi.*

Page 1 photograph: *Detail of a crested mansard roofline from the post-Civil War era in Red Hook, New York.*

Page 2 photograph: *A regal Tuscan villa with French Empire roofline and detailing from Portland, Maine.*

Published by
CHARTWELL BOOKS, INC.
A division of BOOK SALES, INC.
114 Northfield Avenue
Edison, New Jersey 08837

Produced by
Saraband Inc., PO Box 0032, Rowayton, CT 06853-0032

Copyright © 1999, Saraband Inc.

Design © Ziga Design

ISBN 0-7858-1117-6

Printed in China

10 9 8 7 6 5 4 3 2 1

For Lorraine and Glenn

Contents

Introduction

The foundations for the Victorian house were laid in Great Britain even before the eighteen-year-old Princess Victoria ascended the throne in 1837. It was a time of new opportunities for social and political mobility, based upon fortunes made as a result of the Industrial Revolution during the previous century. Despite the stigma still attached to "new" money made in trade or industry, rather than inherited through one's landed or titled forebears, the son of a manufacturer in the textile industry could aspire to become prime minister, as did Sir Robert Peel.

To attain membership in the landed gentry, one had to build a country house designed by a well-known architect like Augustus W.N. Pugin (1812–52) or Sir Charles Barry (1795–1860). In Sir Robert Peel's case, it was his father, the *nouveau riche* Sir Robert Peel the elder, who first built a country house—Drayton Manor, in Staffordshire—about 1830, retaining the services of Sir Robert Smirke, the architect of the British Museum. As Roger Dixon and Stefan Muthesius, the authors of *Victorian Architecture*, point out, domestic architecture was the visible expression of Victorian Britain's social

Above: *A handsome Gothic Revival-style gable, with trefoil window and elegant tracery, on the Justin Morrill House in Strafford, Vermont.*

Previous pages: *The Christopher Gallagher House in Cape May, New Jersey, a National Historic Landmark city with some 600 queenly Victorians.*

A Queen Anne Revival-style turret with conical "witch's cap" roof topped by a finial graces a San Francisco townhouse.

structure: "The house not only reflected the social position of its occupant: it could also suggest the social position to which he aspired. The simpler houses show architectural features copied from the houses of the social class immediately above, and a feature can thus be traced as it makes its way down the social scale in a generation or two from ducal country house to artisan's cottage."

Another case in point is that of the Duke of Sutherland, whose immense fortune was derived from the nation's coal mines. The Neoclassical Greek and Roman styles that were inherited from the eighteenth century were already becoming unfashionable when the duke embarked upon his career as a castlemaker with the help of Sir Charles Barry, who did much of his work in the still-popular Italian Renaissance style. Barry designed no fewer than four palatial residences for the Duke of Sutherland, including Trentham Hall, Staffordshire; Cliveden, Buckinghamshire; Dunrobin Castle, in Scotland; and the imposing Stafford House (now Lancaster House), in London—the requisite townhouse for the London social season.

Queen Victoria herself appreciated the Italian Renaissance style and chose it for Osborne House, her retreat on the Isle of Wight. Designed for her by her husband, Prince Albert of Saxe-Coburg, and architect/builder Thomas Cubitt in the Italian Villa style (1845), the house has both public and private wings, with stucco facing and square, flat-roofed bracketed towers placed asymmetrically for a picturesque effect. While Osborne House far exceeds North American notions of the ideal in domestic tranquillity, it was comparatively modest for a reigning monarch. Houses not dissimilar were being built on a speculative basis in London's Belgravia Square by Cubitt and his brothers, Lewis and William, at the same time.

However, at mid-century, most country-house aspirants favored such native styles as the English Gothic and the Elizabethan. Perhaps the pre-eminent example of the former is Scarisbrick Hall at Ormskirk, in Lancashire, remodeled by Augustus W.N. Pugin for wealthy landowner Charles Scarisbrick. Pugin's deep knowledge of medieval buildings resulted in a Gothic manor house that was complete in every detail. Pugin himself said of the romantic Great Hall: "As regards the hall, I have nailed my colors to the mast—a bay window, high open roof, two good fireplaces, a great sideboard, screen, minstrel gallery—*all or none.* I will not sell myself to do a wretched thing."

Another country-house architect whose ideas on comfort, style and suitability would resonate across the Atlantic was Robert Kerr (1823–1904). His influential book *The Gentleman's House; or How to Plan English Residences, from the Parsonage to the Palace* (1864) was studied eagerly by British, American and Canadian architects alike. Palaces were in limited demand in North America, except among financial and industrial titans like the Vanderbilts and the Morgans, but Victorian notions of good order, healthful location, and spacious rooms and grounds found a receptive audience among the rapidly growing middle class.

The phrase "a man's home is his castle" took on new meaning in the tree-lined suburban enclaves that were emerging in Eastern Seaboard cities like New York, Boston, Philadelphia, Charleston and Savannah, Georgia. They would extend to burgeoning Chicago and Milwaukee later in the century, while newly rich miners, merchants, industrialists and lumber barons would exhibit their affluence from Nevada's Virginia City to Seattle, San Francisco, Los Angeles and Victoria, British Columbia.

The immediate dilemma faced by the person commissioning an impressive Victorian house was much like that described by the British architect Robert Kerr in writing about his clients—the bewildering variety of styles from which to choose.

Quite often the would-be homeowner was at a loss, venturing only to ask for an ample house "in no style at all—except the comfortable style, if there be one." To which the architect responds: "Sir, you are the paymaster, and must therefore be pattern-master; you choose the style of your house just as you choose the build of your hat;—you can have *Classical*, columnar or non-columnar,...rural or civil or indeed palatial; you can have *Elizabethan* in equal variety; *Renaissance* ditto; or, not to notice minor modes, *Medieval* in any one of many periods and many phases,—old English, French, German, Belgian, Italian and more."

In fact, these styles, or variations thereof, all had their day in the sun during the eclectic North American Victorian era, which lasted for years after Queen Victoria's death in 1901, ending a reign of sixty-four years. However, a brief overview shows four distinct stages in the trans-Atlantic development of the style, beginning with the period 1800–25. This was the last phase of the Federal era, which had drawn originally on Renaissance classical models adopted during the reigns of Kings George I, II, III and IV (1714–1830). After the Revolutionary War, the new United States had moved away from Georgian models into styles that drew more directly upon ancient Roman prototypes, as exemplified by the domed Virginia State Capitol at Richmond (1786), by architect and future president Thomas Jefferson. His model was the Augustan temple in Nimes, France (16 BC), called Maison Carrée, which he had studied on his European travels as a statesman. His style, called Jeffersonian Classicism, was especially popular in the Southern states and served as the template for many of the elegant prebellum plantation houses, including his own Virginia estate, Monticello.

Jefferson died in 1826, just as the Greek Revival became the reigning style in American architecture. Its ascendance began with the British-American architect Benjamin H. Latrobe, who built the nation's first major Greek Revival structure, Philadelphia's Bank of Pennsylvania, in 1801. Its main source of inspiration was the Parthenon at Athens (432 BC). Recent archaeological discoveries had provided a direct path to classical antiquity, rather than the roundabout way of the Renaissance styles, and Americans were especially enamored with the Greek style

Above: *The nation's best-known house in the rare Exotic Revival style is Olana, a masterful Moorish castle designed by the Hudson River School painter Frederick Edwin Church and architect Calvert Vaux during the 1870s.*

Right: *Italianate detailing and Palladian windows combine harmoniously to enhance a Midwestern vernacular frame house.*

because of its associations with democracy. By 1830 most new public buildings boasted pediments, columned porticoes and friezes like those of the nation's classical capital, Washington, D.C. There, architect and engineer Robert Mills, a student of Latrobe's, worked with James Hoban on the White House and other influential buildings, including townhouses, churches and federal commissions like the fireproof Records Building (1826) in his native Charleston, South Carolina. Many modest vernacular houses were updated with small entry porches of columnar form, with and without pediments. Standard details of the style were published in carpenters' and builders' manuals, and local craftsmen, as well as architects, combined them freely with such Roman features as domes and vaults. The Roman influence would become especially popular in the late nineteenth century, with the ascendance of the Shingle style and Richardsonian Romanesque, a style that was named for gifted architect Henry Hobson Richardson.

The Greek Revival's main competitor was the picturesque Gothic Revival style, imported from England in its early form during the 1830s. A.W.N. Pugin had published his views on the advantages of medieval over classical architecture in *Contrasts* (1836). He made a strong case for residential designs that conformed to the natural contours of the land and the owner's needs and plans for the use of the building. It was an early statement of the theory "form follows function," but the form looked back to Gothic antecedents and the craftsmanship of an earlier day. Many architects, critics and observers, notably England's John Ruskin, also believed that the rigid demands of classical form imposed artificial constraints that should be thrown off in favor of a more personal picturesque style. All this was music to Victorian ears, and several major North American architects embraced the Gothic Revival style to the exclusion of all others.

Among the most influential exponents of the emergent Gothic Revival style were architects Alexander Jackson Davis and Andrew Jackson Downing, a gifted writer and landscape designer. Davis created several imposing Gothic mansions, including Lyndhurst, in Tarrytown, New York (1838, altered 1864–65), and the William Rotch House in New Bedford, Massachusetts (1846). Since few people could afford these masonry mansions, Downing's book *Cottage Residences* (1842) offered picturesque wooden alternatives for the middle-income family. They included A.J. Davis's design for "a Cottage-Villa in a Rural Gothic Style," with diamond-paned bay windows; tall, thin brick chimneys with ornamental chimney pots; and elaborately carved bargeboards under steep gables. In these prototypes, scroll-sawn wooden trim, later called "gingerbread," replaced expensive stone tracery, giving rise to the term Carpenter's Gothic.

Coincident with the Gothic Revival style was a new type of wooden construction called balloon framing. An armature of continuous wooden members was assembled rapidly with machine-made nails, making it possible to build a strong structure with far less labor than involved in traditional post-and-beam construction. Precut lumber and cheaper, mass-produced materials contributed to the building boom, especially in the West, where new towns sprang up almost overnight as Eastern railroad lines extended. Many pattern books featured variations on the Gothic Revival cottage, as did A.J. Downing's second book, *The Architecture of Country Houses* (1850). According to Lester Walker, the author of *American Shelter* (Overlook Press, 1981): "Downing's houses were distinguished by steep roof slopes, balconies, porches, window gables and deep shadows made by projecting roofs. He was after the ideal building—the house that suited the owner's needs and the land best. He saw the picturesque as a natural style that could provide 'true, honest and functional' architecture yet fit the landscape in

Left: *A lavishly carved frieze in Victorian San Francisco.*

a romantic way." Other architects, designers and writers contributed to the growing list of readily available pattern books, which included Gervase Wheeler's *Rural Homes* (1851) and Calvert Vaux's *Villas and Cottages* (1857).

The Italianate style, inspired by Renaissance models, flourished from the mid-nineteenth century until about 1885. Its characteristics included a square cupola or tower surmounting a low-pitched roof; wide eaves with decorative, sometimes intricately carved, brackets below; and tall, narrow windows, usually arched or ornamented with U-shaped hood molds, and often ranked in twos and threes. The house plan was frequently square or rectangular.

The Tuscan-villa style, with a square tower where two wings met, was popular for large country and suburban houses, and Italianate townhouses made the most of narrow city lots. Their flat or low-pitched roofs were invisible from the street side due to their wide bracketed eaves. Many commercial buildings, as well as houses, were built in this style during the late nineteenth century and can still be seen in small towns all over the continent.

Another distinctive Victorian style, often combined with the Italianate, was the French Second Empire, which became fashionable during the reign of Napoleon III (1851–70). Its hallmark was the distinctive mansard roof—a dual-pitched hip roof with dormer windows on the steep lower slope and sometimes with convex or concave curved planes. This decorative style featured elaborate door and window surrounds, iron cresting above bracketed eaves and along the roofline, and one- or two-story porches with balustrades above and below. Double entry doors were favored, with handsome hardware, and glazing above. Façade openings were usually ranked in threes, and some examples have central cupolas or towers. The style became so popular in the United States after the Civil War that it is often called the General Grant style, for the military hero's presidency (1869–77).

The indigenous Stick style was taken up after the publication of A.J. Downing's *Architecture of Country Carpentry Made Easy* (1858). It was transitional between the enduring Gothic Revival and the triumphant Queen Anne Revival, which would become the reigning style in domestic architecture until after the turn of the century. All three of these styles featured adaptations of medieval English building traditions. Closely related and contemporaneous was the High Victorian Gothic style popularized by John Ruskin in such books as *The Stones of Venice*, which drew upon Italian rather than English Gothic traditions. Ruskinian Gothic, as it is often called, had a strong influence on Queen Anne Revival houses in the use of contrasting surface materials called polychrome—patterned brick, stucco, shingles and other features that made color intrinsic to the building. While High Victorian Gothic structures were most often churches and public buildings of stone construction, their principles were influential on wooden houses in which multiple details were highlighted by contrasting paint colors, as seen in the restored "painted ladies" of San

Below: *An eclectic Queen Anne façade combines classical arches and dentils with unusual Stick-style gable trim.*

Francisco and other North American cities and towns. In lieu of slate tiles and cut stone, they achieved their multitextured effects with alternating bands of shingles, appliqué work, terra-cotta panels and other readily available materials. With its spacious porches; high-pitched, multilevel roofs; and delightful turrets, towers and ornamental spoolwork, the Queen Anne Revival style was both the high point and the epitome of the eclectic Victorian styles.

Many of the asymmetrical Queen Annes were executed in the Shingle style, which became popular for resort architecture during the late 1800s. A major influence on this style was the gifted American architect Henry Hobson Richardson, who had studied at the *École des Beaux Arts* in Paris. Many of his rambling resort houses were clad in shingles designed to unite their disparate elements, and featured deeply recessed arched entryways and shingled or stonework piers as porch supports. Richardson's unique style found its fullest expression in the Romanesque style that bears his name, as seen in Boston's Trinity Church and Chicago's John Glessner House, completed in 1887, a year after the architect's untimely death at the age of forty-seven.

The plates that follow include examples of the rich interiors that reflected the wide-ranging interests of the growing, upwardly mobile middle class. Natural history became a passion during the nineteenth century, and inspired both collections and ornamentation including seashells, botanical motifs, butterflies, exotic animal forms and a host of others. House-proud owners spared no expense for elaborate lamps, chandeliers, drapery, carpets, tiling and furniture. Elaborately carved woodwork, elegant conservatories and imported textiles contributed to the comfort and style of these exuberant dwellings, which retain their power to charm and delight long after they were originally constructed. It is fortunate that the ever-growing interest in Victorian architecture has rescued so many of these houses from demolition and neglect and restored them to their rightful place in the ongoing history of North American architecture.

Classical Influences

The Victorian fascination with the long ago and the far away expressed itself during the early 1800s in what Americans call the Greek Revival and Canadians, the Neoclassical style. Imported from Europe several decades after it became fashionable there—primarily for major public buildings and aristocratic marble mansions—the Greek Revival struck deeper roots in the New World, especially in the United States.

The influence of Thomas Jefferson, classical scholar, architect and statesman, was imprinted on the new national capital on the Potomac River, and within a few years Greek porticoes adorned buildings from Virginia to New England and eastern Canada. Perhaps equally important in the ascendance of the Greek style was the English-born architect Benjamin H. Latrobe, a friend and colleague of Jefferson's. The houses and commercial buildings that Latrobe designed drew directly upon the Athenian Parthenon and the Choragic Monument of Lysicrates. He modeled his Baltimore Cathedral (1806) on the Pantheon at Paris (although he prepared an alternate design in the emergent Gothic Revival style, which is discussed in the following chapter).

Previous pages:
An elegant two-story Grecian bay on a Charleston, South Carolina, mansion.

A classical pediment centered on a pedestal bearing a pineapple— a traditional sign of hospitality—in Newport, Rhode Island.

Since the Renaissance, the public buildings of ancient Greece and Rome had set the standard for architectural beauty, with their foursquare or rectangular shapes, bold columned façades and harmony of balanced forms. They did not conform to the landscape, but dominated it, standing above their surroundings in stark white splendor (most of their colorful friezes had long since worn away). Jefferson was enthralled by the great Augustan temple built in Gaul (later France) by the Romans in 16 BC, and its influence is seen in the gilded rotunda of his Richmond, Virginia, State Capitol building and in the classical campus he designed for the University of Virginia at Charlottesville, both major contributions in the timeline of world architecture.

Greco-Roman associations with the ideals of democracy and republicanism had a strong appeal for the newly independent United States, despite the fact that very few workaday citizens of ancient Greece or Rome had actually participated in their governments. It was enough that such principles had been embodied in the Declaration of Independence and the United States Constitution and were being expressed in stone along the well-planned avenues of Washington, D.C. In fact, many observers believe that American Grecian buildings are equal to, and sometimes superior to, those of the Old World. Briton John Maass, in *The Gingerbread Age* (Rinehart & Co, 1957), comments that: "The country was studded with 'temples,' from court houses down to bird boxes. Every carpenter ploughed, tongued and grooved the Antique into cornices....We have been taught to regard 'Greek' and 'beautiful' as one and the same, and the Greek Revival in America has left a treasure of beauty. There are no lovelier houses anywhere than the grand plantations of Louisiana, ringed with tall wooden columns. Shaded Main Street in Nantucket town, with its white Grecian homes, must be one of the most beautiful streets in the world."

It was late eighteenth-century steel engravings of the recently excavated volcano-buried ruins of Pompeii and Herculaneum that inspired the Greek Revival in Europe. Preserved almost intact, the rediscovered splendor of the Italian cities showed the refined monumentality of the original buildings, as compared to the Renaissance models of a much later date. When the Greek Revival reached North America, the style first became popular in the South, where it was admirably suited to creating a sense of serene grandeur while also taking advantage of riverside breezes and reflecting the hot glare of the sun. Rising first along the James River in Virginia, the Southern plantation house, as enshrined in Margaret Mitchell's Civil War novel *Gone With the Wind*, soon spread as far south as Georgia and west to the Mississippi River, where cotton was king during the 1850s. Natchez and Vicksburg, Mississippi, are famous for their elegant plantation and townhouses, and Fort Smith, Arkansas, an early gateway to the West, has many examples in its Belle Grove Historic District.

Meanwhile, the Greek Revival had spread to Atlantic Canada, New England and the mid-Atlantic states, where many rectangular colonial houses were refashioned so that the gable end, with its elegant portico and pediment, faced the street for all to admire. In more modest vernacular forms, the style had reached the trans-Mississippi West before 1850. Interior decoration reflected its influence in fluted columns flanking parlor doors, botanical ornamentation inspired by Mediterranean acanthus leaves and stylized honeysuckle (called anthemion), and table legs in the form of Greek lyres.

Many important Greek Revival houses were built in coastal cities from Boston to New York during the 1830s. The style's popularity was boosted by an 1827 watercolor by Alexander Jackson Davis (who studied as an artist with Rembrandt Peale before taking up architecture), which includes a view of the Philip Hone House, owned by the mayor of New York for the term 1825 to 1826. Imposing colonnaded rowhouses were built in Manhattan and Brooklyn Heights, and Davis designed a Greek Revival mansion with a Roman dome for John Cox Stevens (1849) near what is now Columbia University. The juxtaposition of Greek and Gothic was seen at Samuel Thompson's Mount Washington, on Washington Heights, where a Grecian temple-style house shared the grounds with a picturesque "rustic Gothic" pavilion, or summerhouse. Other classical residences were built along the lower Hudson River, including that of the painter John James Audubon.

In eastern Canada, the Greek Revival style was adopted from the 1820s to the 1850s for public buildings as the population and economy expanded at a rapid rate. Many homes of the period were adorned with Greek Revival detailing, including pediments, pilasters, decorative fretwork and balustrades.

Throughout the nineteenth century, classical models inspired American architects, including Henry Hobson Richardson, who founded the nation's first major style independent of European models. Known as Richardsonian Romanesque, his massive, round-arched buildings were constructed primarily of rock-faced (rusticated) masonry, with deeply recessed entryways; short, powerful piers instead of columns; and blocky towers of rounded, square, or octagonal form. His influence was felt across the nation, from such late-century buildings as the Gardner Museum of Architecture and Design (formerly the public library) in Quincy, Illinois, to San Francisco mansions built and painted to resemble faceted stone.

Romanesque forms also appeared in Richardson's Shingle-style resort houses. Architectural historian Vincent Scully, who named the style, describes it as "magisterial, pervasive and national" until the late 1880s (*The Architecture of the American Summer*, Rizzoli, 1989). Its principal exponents, besides Richardson, included the fashionable East Coast firm of McKim, Mead and White; William Ralph Emerson; Peabody and Stearns; and John Calvin Stevens. The young Frank Lloyd Wright was deeply influenced by Richardson's work, as seen in his Shingle-style home/studio in Oak Park, Illinois, and in many of his late-century designs for clients in suburban Chicago and other Midwestern cities. An excellent example was designed in San Francisco by Samuel Newsom in 1892, with characteristic shingle-clad pitched roofs, broad gables and multiple dormers.

After the Philadelphia Centennial of 1876, the Classical styles were reprised into the early 1900s in the style called both Neoclassical and Colonial Revival. It combined the symmetrical features of earlier Georgian and Federal houses with one- or two-story porticoes, triple Palladian windows, hipped roofs and graceful swan's-neck pediments. Here, too, the eclectic firm of McKim, Mead and White led the way in a quest to impose order on the architectural scene, which had been dominated by a myriad of picturesque styles, beginning with the Gothic Revival, since the 1840s. According to *The Story of Architecture*, by P.L. Waterhouse and R.A. Cordingly (B.T. Batsford, 1950): "[The firm] produced a great body of work, mainly Renaissance in type, but including Roman, Romanesque, Byzantine...so fresh and polished in style and so admirably adapted to the circumstances of the New World that they appear as distinctively American."

Above: *Shirley Plantation, built near Williamsburg, Virginia, during the 1700s in the classical Georgian style, features a two-story portico with simple pediment.*

Opposite: *A tasteful Grecian entry porch with fluted columns adorns a Federal-style brick house on Woodstock, Vermont's, River Street.*

Georgian and Greek Revival

The enduring effect of the classical styles favored in England and France as the New World was being colonized is apparent across the North American continent. The prevailing standard of beauty before the advent of the romantic nineteenth century was that of ancient Greece and Rome. Balance, symmetry and harmony of proportions dominated early North American architecture once housing evolved from simple shelter for survival's sake to a form of personal and communal expression. Ornamentation was minimal and restrained, and convenience was often sacrificed to conformity, as preordained forms molded the use of interior spaces. As the Georgian, Federal and Greek Revival styles succeeded one another into the early nineteenth century, new insights into the classical aesthetic resulted

in freer adaptations of existing forms to suit national and local needs. The early Georgian townhouse, farmhouse and plantation moved from Renaissance-inspired interpretations like Palladianism to bolder, simpler forms based on Greco-Roman originals, as disclosed by discoveries in archaeology and cultural history. An emergent sense of national identity made architects, builders and craftsmen more confident in their adaptations of time-honored styles.

Opposite: *Magnolia Plantation, a prebellum Greek Revival estate house in Natchez, Mississippi, with an elegant portico of fluted Ionic columns.*

Above: *A Tuscaloosa, Alabama, plantation house with a full-height portico raised on an arcade, decorative ironwork balustrades and double staircase.*

Overleaf: *Colonnade Row on New York City's Lafayette Street was designed by Alexander Jackson Davis (1833) as a Greek Revival rowhouse of nine residences screened by Corinthian columns of Westchester marble.*

Developed by Seth Geer, the townhouses were mockingly referred to as "Geer's Folly." However, the residences proved successful with the public. Notable tenants include Washington Irving and Charles Dickens.

Left: *During the early Victorian era, many a sturdy vernacular farmhouse was embellished by Greek Revival detailing like this pediment and modest porch.*

Below: *An elegant clapboard townhouse in Stonington, Connecticut, built by Gordon Trumbull in 1840, boasts Greek Revival corner pilasters, Ionic entry columns and an atypical cupola above the cornice line.*

Opposite: *A dentiled Greek Revival pediment with an elaborate window surround supports an Italianate cupola in this eclectic gable treatment from Red Hook, New York.*

Shingle Style and Variations

As Victorian houses—both those designed for year-round occupancy and seasonal or resort homes—gradually became more asymmetrical and rambling in form, new modes of cladding and ornamentation emerged to unify disparate elements. With affinities to both the Romanesque and Queen Anne styles, the Shingle style became popular, especially for resort houses, about 1885. It originated on the East Coast and often combined unpainted siding, which was allowed to weather naturally, with rough-

cut shingles—machine-made, but reminiscent of New England colonial architecture. Romanesque elements included squat towers, exaggerated arches, rusticated masonry foundations, hipped Norman-style roofs and an emphasis on the horizontal rather than the vertical. Often called "seaside," referring to the Atlantic coast, Shingle-style houses spread across the continent to the Middle West and, in isolated examples, to the West Coast by the turn of the century, when their popularity with the public waned.

Left: *A Shingle-style house with Queen Anne detailing on the still-fashionable resort of Block Island, Rhode Island. Raised slightly on piers for coolness, it commands the scenic view from every side.*

Below: *The Shingle style often incorporated a gambrel roof of colonial form, as seen in this suburban example from South Orange, New Jersey.*

Above: *A handsomely modernized Shingle-style house in Medina, Ohio, remains true to its origins in its deeply recessed porches, simple wall and roof cladding, gable and turret.*

Left: *Cut and incised ornamentation decorates the exterior of a charming shingled Vermont Victorian.*

Right: *Appliquéd Eastlake-style detail adorns the second story of an eclectic country house in rural Lime Rock, Connecticut.*

Below: *As seen in the detail at right, this late-century house in Connecticut combines Shingle-style with Queen Anne features, including the short polygonal tower with bellcast roof and the large arched entryway to the porch, with its spindle- and spoolwork ornamentation.*

Richardsonian Romanesque

Both American and Canadian architects had begun to experiment with the emergent pre-Gothic Romanesque style as early as the 1840s, primarily for imposing public buildings of masonry construction. However, it was not until the advent of Henry Hobson Richardson's work of the 1870s and '80s that the Romanesque style took on the unique imprint that it bears today. His buildings were characterized by rock-faced masonry walls with bold arches and lintels and short, thick towers that conveyed a sense of solidity. The thrust was horizontal, with transomed windows grouped in bands and rock walls laid in irregular courses. Richardson and his followers favored simple silhouettes, gabled roofs with minimal overhang and Norman-style hipped roofs with stout towers at the corners, or where two wings intersected. Large round-arched entries were emphasized by segmental surrounds of brick or stone, and deeply set façade openings created shadows that increased the massive quality of the masonry forms. Richardson's influence is seen in the work of such pre-eminent American architects as Frank Lloyd Wright and Louis Sullivan, whose early careers overlapped with his own. Sadly, Richardson died at the age of only forty-seven, leaving a relatively small body of work that is even more highly esteemed now than it was in his lifetime.

Left: *A Pittsburgh, Pennsylvania, landmark combines Romanesque massing with stepped gables characteristic of the medieval style of the Low Countries.*

Overleaf: *The turreted profile of the tower at the great Henry Ford estate, Fair Lane, in Dearborn, Michigan. Designed by Pittsburgh architect William H. Van Tine, the residence was constructed with limestone from Marblehead, Ohio.*

Below: *Richardson's major residential design, the John J. Glessner House in Chicago (1886–87), was completed a year after his death. It features rugged rock-faced walls, recessed windows and short, massive chimneys that emphasize the horizontal lines of the building.*

Above: *An imposing Romanesque corbel in the form of a stylized lion's head adorns the façade of the Newman Center in Toronto.*

Left: *A sturdy Romanesque townhouse from Canada with Queen Anne detailing added to the upper levels.*

Opposite: *The quintessential Romanesque tower, with arched openings delineated by heavy, rough-faced stonework and alternating bands of brick that maintain the horizontal profile.*

Above: *The Italian Renaissance palazzo The Breakers, built between 1892 and 1895 by Richard Morris Hunt as a summer residence for Cornelius Vanderbilt II at a cost of $7 million.*

Right: *Ochre Court, in the French Renaissance style, was among the first ornaments of Newport's exclusive Ochre Point, named for the color of its native stone. The property is now owned by Salve Regina College.*

Late-Century Renaissance Revival

The classical influence reigned over Newport, Rhode Island's, Gilded Age as the resort of the country's untitled aristocracy—the rich and famous. Second- and third-generation scions of the railroad, shipping and financial tycoons retained Beaux-Arts architects like Richard Morris Hunt to re-create the grandeur of the French and Italian Renaissance in multimillion-dollar "cottages" overlooking Narragansett Bay. These eclectic mansions demanded both scholarship and imagination on the part of the architect and landscape designers in addition to cadres of stonecutters, woodcarvers, masons and interior designers to execute the finished product.

The Gothic Revival

When the early Gothic Revival style first manifested itself in North America during the 1830s, there was little to suggest that its influence would become the most pervasive of all the nineteenth-century styles. It would have a far more lasting effect than, say, the relatively transient French Second Empire style of the 1870s and '80s, and would become the dominant style for church architecture well into the following century. Architects were ready to free themselves of the constraints imposed by traditional classical styles, including the Greek Revival, which squeezed internal living space into a boxlike form that was often more imposing than comfortable.

The new picturesque style imported from England was endorsed by such eminent British architects as Augustus W.N. Pugin and J.C. Loudon, the author of *Encyclopedia of Cottage, Farm and Villa Architecture and Furniture*, published in 1833. Proponents like John Nash and Humphrey Repton saw the house as an integral part of the landscape and encouraged a rambling, asymmetrical style that conformed to the owner's needs and the local topography. Its prototypes were such late-Gothic manor houses as

Previous pages:
Steeply sloped gables with intricately carved finials enhance the vertical thrust of the Gothic Revival Sellers Carnahan house in Pittsburgh, Pennsylvania.

Elegant tracery and arched windows ornament a picturesque Carpenter's Gothic cottage in Grosse Ile, Michigan.

Horham Hall (1502), in Essex, composed of various peaked and gabled forms grouped together in romantic profusion, with triple windows detailed in the manner of Gothic cathedrals.

Among the American architects who professed the new style with contagious enthusiasm were Alexander Jackson Davis and landscape designer Andrew Jackson Downing, editor of *The Horticulturist.* He was the first to publicize the style, in his *Treatise and Theory of Landscape Gardening Adapted to North America* (1841). In its preface, Downing stated that "Within the last ten years, especially, the evidence of the growing wealth and prosperity of our citizens has become apparent in the great increase of elegant cottages and villa residences on the banks of our noble rivers, along our rich valleys, and wherever nature seems to invite us by her rich and varied charms."

Downing's reference to "noble rivers" was especially pertinent to his own native Hudson River Valley, where he objected strongly to the cubical white Greek temples that he saw as intrusive upon the landscape. In his next book, *Cottage Residences* (1842), he published detailed house plans for wooden houses in the Gothic mode, many of them designed by his friend and mentor A.J. Davis. The book was so popular that it went through numerous printings, as did its successor *The Architecture of Country Houses* (1850). Vertical board-and-batten siding, ornate double chimneys and accentuated rafter brackets were features of the cottage style, which also brought the front porch into prominence in northern climates, as a seasonal, semiprivate outdoor "room." (Prior to this time, porches had been used mainly on Southern-style houses for their cooling effect.)

The Victorian love of ornament first had full play in the Gothic Revival style, especially in the indigenous form called Carpenter's Gothic. The invention of the steam-powered scroll saw, and the development of rapidly constructed balloon framing, contributed to the rapid spread of Gothic villas and cottages lavishly adorned with "gingerbread" trim in the form of brackets, porch railings, trelliswork and gable-end bargeboards. This wooden tracery was much easier to produce than the hand-carved stonework of Gothic Revival mansions executed for wealthy clients by architects like Davis and Richard Upjohn. For every such masonry estate house, with its stately towers and ranks of pointed windows, hundreds of colorful, quirky vernacular houses sprang up, as if to confirm Downing's assertion that "When smiling lawns and tasteful cottages begin to embellish a country, we know that order and culture are established."

Architectural pattern books were not the only source of the decorative scrollwork and curlicues identified with North American Gothic. Both local carpenters and sawmill owners designed their own inventive variations and advertised them to prospective homebuilders: "All Kinds of Scroll Sawing and Wood Turning. Architectural Carving, Done to Order at Short Notice." The results may be seen in endless variety from the New England states to northern California, the Pacific Northwest and Victoria, British Columbia.

Examples of the style include Springside, built during the 1850s by a Poughkeepsie, New York, brewer and admired by a contemporary in extravagant terms as "a lasting monument to the genius of Downing and the liberality and taste of its proprietor, Mr. Vassar, who with a generosity equal to his taste permits the public to enjoy the charms he has created." These charms included a pink-and-white confection with ornamental iron fencing—the gate lodge below the main house—and carefully tended gardens rife with urns and twining vines. A.J. Davis did most of his work in New York State, exemplified by Lyndhurst, an elegant stone mansion in Tarrytown, but the popularity of his book *Rural Residences* (1838) also created a demand for his services in New England and Virginia, while his designs were implemented in Atlantic Canada and on the West Coast long before his death in 1892.

Richard Upjohn, an English cabinetmaker, emigrated to the United States to become one of the nation's most distinguished architects of Gothic Revival houses and churches. The handsome house known as Kingscote, in Newport, Rhode Island, was designed in the late 1830s for a Savannah resident named George Noble Jones, at the time when Newport was becoming a fashionable resort for wealthy New Yorkers and other summer visitors. Another New England landmark is Woodstock, Connecticut's, Roseland Cottage, the country house of businessman Henry Bowen, designed by the English architect Joseph Collins Wells on a lavish scale that includes flamboyant gables topped with finials, diamond-paned casement windows, decorative bays and oriels, and serpentine bargeboards. The house was constructed by master carpenter Edwin Eaton of Connecticut and is now owned by the Society for the Preservation of New England Antiquities.

Southeastern Gothic cottages of great charm include Ethridge House (1853), in Sparta, Georgia; the James Sledge House (c. 1860), in Athens, Georgia; and the Zebulon Latimer House, built for a transplanted Connecticut Yankee in Wilmington, North Carolina, in 1852. Even Florida, which did not achieve statehood until 1846, took up the Gothic Revival in the early resort town of Fernandina Beach and in prosperous north-central Lake City.

The Gothic Revival became extremely popular in the Midwest, where vernacular examples are found throughout Indiana, Illinois, Wisconsin and adjacent states. Former president Harry S. Truman grew up in a rambling gabled Victorian in Independence, Missouri. In New Orleans, ornamental ironwork often served as, or augmented, the decorative trim on stylish townhouses in the Old French Quarter and the emergent Garden District. Before the American Civil War, an especially ornate variation of Carpenter's Gothic, called Steamboat Gothic, evolved along the Mississippi River and its major tributaries, including the Ohio and the Missouri. The style took its name from decorative paddlewheel steamers like the *Delta Queen*, which were embellished with intricate wooden railings, scroll-sawn brackets and metal smokestack detailing.

The apex of the Gothic Revival is seen in the polychrome buildings of the High Victorian Gothic style, beginning about 1875. This phase was influenced primarily by the English cultural historian John Ruskin, who advocated revival of the Gothic style of northern Italy, rather than England. His most influential book on the subject was *The Seven Lamps of Architecture* (1849), which was the exemplar for many churches and public buildings, as well as expensive residences incorporating ornamental pressed brick, carved stone, stucco and patterned shinglework. The influence of what is often called Ruskinian Gothic can be traced in the Queen Anne Revival style, as described in chapter 4. Frank Furness was the acknowledged master of this eclectic style. Notable examples of his work occur principally in his native Philadelphia, where he undertook some 600 projects. Unfortunately, many have been demolished, but his landmark Pennsylvania Academy of Art (1876) has been preserved intact.

Asymmetrical Massing

A hallmark of the picturesque Gothic Revival was its radical break with the symmetrical cube-shaped and rectangular "boxes" of the classical styles. The new villas, cottages, even "castles," tended to ramble at will over the site, thrusting out a bay window here, an unexpected gable there, an ornate chimney pot, an arched "eyebrow" dormer with a slight flare at either end. The roofline usually had a steep slope, originally designed to shed rain and snow from medieval thatched roofs, and a prominent front-facing gable was almost *de rigueur*.

Dormers sprouted steep triangular roofs that were often trimmed with wooden gingerbread, and carved and turned finials sprang from the rooflines to increase the sense of verticality. Porches were no longer confined to "front" or "back," but turned corners and ascended in the form of irregular balconies rimmed with decorative balustrades. The Gothic style could be—and was—interpreted in a myriad of structural and ornamental forms, from the stately English-style manor house to the stickwork detailing that recalled medieval half-timbering.

Opposite: *A roomy cottage—formerly the lighthouse keeper's quarters—with an unusual double-sloped roofline and a decorative multiflued chimney, on Oregon's Heceta Head.*

Above: *A charming Canadian farmhouse updated in the Gothic mode in New London, Prince Edward Island.*

Carpenter's Gothic

Both the United States and Canada were graced with carpenters of exceptional skill, who could identify native woods and their various properties by sight—even by smell. They tailored their buildings to use each kind of wood to best advantage, whether for durability, workability, or strength. The invention of steam-powered scroll saws and the profusion of pattern books and builder's manuals gave their skills free reign, as seen in the beauty and variety of their detailing. Many improvised freely from existing models to become artists in woodwork, while building suppliers enjoyed a booming business in prefabricated trim sold to the prospective homebuilder at moderate cost. The sky became the limit for intricate, imaginative detailing in the picturesque mode.

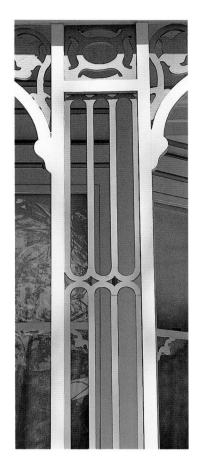

Opposite: *Seaside resorts embraced the Gothic Revival for its picturesque qualities, as seen in the Joseph Hall House in Cape May, New Jersey (1868).*

Left: *The porch trim on the Joseph Hall House (opposite) combines organic forms with vertical, rectilinear woodwork.*

Below: *An intricate bargeboard frames an attractive balcony at Oak Bluffs Camp Ground, on Martha's Vineyard, Massachusetts.*

Above: *The charming Stratton Mare House (c. 1860) in Cape May, New Jersey, features a steep central gable and delicate tracery.*

Opposite: *The shadows cast by curvilinear and pointed forms contribute to the visual interest of this rhythmic façade.*

Right: *A delicate finial unites the ribbonlike tracery on this Victorian gable at the Ryan Premises in Bonavista, Newfoundland. The squat chimney is a contrasting element.*

Above: *Flattened Tudor arches outline the full-length porch of a Gothic cottage at Hastings-on-Hudson, New York.*

Right: *Detail of the cottage above, a quatrefoil gable ornament framed by trefoil tracery.*

Opposite: *Frosted in lacelike tracery, Cape May's Eldridge Johnson House (1882), a side-hall cottage, resembles a wedding cake.*

Above: *Speculative builders filled town and city blocks with similar designs that were personalized by eager home buyers, as seen in New Jersey's seaside community of Cape May.*

Right: *A summer cottage in Ocean Grove, New Jersey, has arches of basket and Moorish form framed in geometric grids of Eastlake inspiration.*

The Stick Style

The mid-nineteenth century saw the advent of the Stick Style, named by architectural historian Vincent Scully. As a style of patterning on vernacular wood-frame houses, it was modeled on English Picturesque prototypes like those designed by J.C. Loudon. As Mr. Scully describes it in his introduction to *The Architecture of the American Summer* (Rizzoli, 1989): "Loudon and others first brought the wooden skeleton to the surface, dominated by the vertical post, and from that moment everything happened very rapidly and with a special social and technological freshness in America. Andrew Jackson Downing and a horde of builders of single-family houses from Maine to California could even achieve the new effects...with vertical planks and battens alone." The distinctive surface embellishments included diagonal braces, ripple effects and repetitive vertical and horizontal moldings.

Opposite: *One of the country's best-known exemplars of the Stick style: the Emlen Physick House (1878) in Cape May, New Jersey, by Frank Furness.*

Above: *Stick-style ornamentation on an imposing Queen Anne—Rose Lawn, in Natchitoches, Louisiana—built at the turn of the century.*

Opposite: *An elegant Gothic oriel with leaded glass in the upper window sashes and stickwork detailing on an imposing stone house in Pittsburgh, Pennsylvania.*

Above: *A romantic Stick-style playhouse built for Josephine Ford on her grandparents' Michigan estate.*

Right: *A decorative gable on an impressive summer home in the fashionable resort of Bar Harbor, Maine.*

Gothic Cottages and Manors

When prosperous tycoons and financiers wanted a house that testified to their success, they retained a well-known architect and provided a lavish budget. Expense was no object to building a medieval castle or manor house on the American Rhine—the Hudson River—along the coasts, or anyplace between where suitable materials and craftsmen could be assembled. Auto barons built castles in Michigan, and brewers in Milwaukee. Iron-and-steel men from Pittsburgh and New York bankers and railroad tycoons vied with one another in the size and opulence of their palatial townhouses and summer places. Their architects included such renowned figures as Richard Upjohn, John Notman, Alexander Jackson Davis, Richard Morris Hunt, Calvert Vaux and Frederick Clarke Withers.

Left: *Detail of a masterful bay window with elegant Gothic tracery at Lyndhurst.*

Above: *Perhaps the greatest house in the Gothic Revival style is Lyndhurst, at Tarrytown, New York, designed by Alexander Jackson Davis in 1838.*

Overlooking the Hudson River and built of brick overlaid with marble from nearby Ossining, New York, the mansion is dominated by a four-story tower.

Above: *The eclectic fifty-two-room Lockwood-Mathews Mansion in Norwalk, Connecticut, was designed by Danish-American architect Detlef Lienau for banker and railroad tycoon LeGrand Lockwood. Constructed between 1864 and 1868, the estate, which was then known as "Elm Park," was sold to Charles D. Mathews in 1876. It is now a museum.*

Below: *Pennsylvania Gothic, as seen in the entryway, arches, bays and tall chimneys of Hawthorne, in Reading.*

Below: *Stepped gables and baroque dormers distinguish the Flemish Gothic Pabst House in Milwaukee, Wisconsin. The three-story mansion was constructed for beer baron Captain Frederik Pabst in 1893.*

Opposite: *Built at a cost of $4 million, with more than 100 rooms, Meadow Brook Hall, in Rochester, Michigan, has diamond-patterned brickwork, thirty-nine medieval-style chimneys and a crenellated tower.*

Above: *The Cotswold-style Edsel and Eleanor Ford mansion in Grosse Pointe Shores, Michigan. The grounds were designed by landscape architect Jens Jensen.*

Overleaf: *Richard Morris Hunt combined French Gothic and Renaissance elements for Biltmore, in Asheville, North Carolina, commissioned by George Washington Vanderbilt in 1890. It took a thousand workmen and almost $5 million to construct the five-acre mansion.*

Right: *An ivy-wreathed globe ornaments a brick pier on the Ford estate.*

Italianate and French Second Empire

Since Italy was the cultural mecca for British, American and Canadian travelers of the nineteenth century, as seen in such novels as Henry James's *The Wings of the Dove*, it is not surprising that the Italianate villa became the pattern of so many North American buildings from the 1830s onward. The early Victorians believed that "architecture is an art in which Italy has no modern rival." As mentioned, Queen Victoria and Prince Albert built one of their two country houses, Osborne, in the elegant villa style, and many of the architects who popularized the Italianate in North America were recent arrivals from Great Britain. They included Gervase Wheeler, John Notman, Richard Upjohn (best known for his Gothic Revival churches) and Calvert Vaux, code-signer with Frederick Law Olmsted of New York City's Central Park.

Previous pages:
A square tower, typical of the Italianate country mansion house style that was popular in the Hudson Valley in mid-century, on the Glenview House, Yonkers, New York. The mansion now serves as the Hudson River Museum of Westchester.

Detail of the imposing wooden bracketed tower above the entrance to Acorn Hall in Morristown, New Jersey.

The most picturesque features of the style are its towers and cupolas, the latter often called belvederes. They were praised as "affording a cool retreat where the breeze blows unmolested and whence a cheerful and extended prospect is commanded." While the square tower, with its bracketed cornice, formed part of the floor plan on a country house with several wings, the cupola was a rooftop ornament introduced mainly for the fun of it on a cube-shaped house with a flat roof. (In the South, and on Octagon houses, the cupola was useful for ventilation.) It formed a delightful "crown" topped by a scrolled finial, and was usually accessed through a trap door (which must have made it attractive to the children of the house as the ideal secret hide-out).

Handsome and well-proportioned, with open ground plans incorporating terraces and loggias, bold moldings and cornices, the Italianate country house set a new standard of beauty for several generations. President Martin Van Buren remodeled his Dutch-colonial style homestead, Lindenwald, at Kinderhook, New York, in the fashionable Renaissance style, with arched Palladian windows, brackets and a balustrated cupola. The original Franklin Delano Roosevelt home at Hyde Park, New York—called Springwood—was designed in the Tuscan-villa style, its sweeping grounds sloping down to the Hudson River. It has since been altered by a neo-Georgian façade. Edith Wharton's novel *Hudson River Bracketed* (a popular name for the style, which flourished in the Hudson Valley) was set in The Willows, modeled on her aunt Elizabeth Jones's mansion, Wyndcliffe, at Rhinebeck, New York, where Wharton spent girlhood summers.

In New Castle, Delaware, an unusual villa with Gothic detailing was built by Augustin Van Kirk for Dr. Allen Lesley about 1855. Baltimore architects Thomas and James Dixon drew up the plans and incorporated such expensive innovations as central heating, gas lights, doorbells, and hot and cold running water. Now known as the Lesley-Travers Mansion, the house has been restored and repainted in pastel shades of peach and blue-green.

One of the most popular house plans in A.J. Downing's *Architecture of Country Houses* was "Villa in the Italian style," for which Richard Upjohn had designed the prototype in 1845. Downing praised this villa, the Edward King House, as "one of the most successful specimens of the Italian style in the United States, [which] unites beauty of form and expression with spacious accommodations." Now serving the City of Newport, Rhode Island, as a social center, the King House inspired a host of imitators, from Baltimore to Detroit and San Francisco.

The symmetrical, cube-shaped Italianate proved equally adaptable, sprouting cupolas in many fanciful styles and, later, rambling verandahs with slender columns and bracketed rooflines. Whether built in wood, in stone, or in brick, like the T.J. Campau residence in Detroit (1869), contemporary accounts attest to the fact that the villa owner "lives in a style becoming his wealth and position."

An 1857 view of New York City's Fifth Avenue south of 36th Street shows blocks of Italianate townhouses. Generically known as brownstones in the nation's larger cities, these attached houses with adapted Renaissance detailing were actually built of brick faced with slabs of sandstone, or freestone. Up to four stories high, most examples have a stairway with balustrade leading to the entrance on the raised first floor, with service areas on the ground floor. The common rooms on the first floor—parlors and dining room—have the highest ceilings, while the upper floors are progressively shorter. Built to serve as substantial single-family housing, most of the urban brownstones have been converted during the twentieth century to apartment and rooming houses; others were demolished during economic booms to make room for lucrative high rises. The plates that follow illustrate both the elegance and variety of the versatile Italianate townhouse. The style peaked in popularity just before the American Civil War and was reprised in more florid and ornate versions by Beaux-Arts architects of the late nineteenth century.

Sharing many features of the Italianate style, and often combined with it, was the French Second Empire style, popularized in Europe by Napoleon III during the 1850s. Its hallmark was the mansard roof, with four steep sides broken by large dormer windows in graceful frames. Its slope could be straight, concave, convex, or a combination of the latter two that formed an S-shaped curve, often topped with filigree iron crestwork.

In Paris, new wings in a grandiose Neo-Renaissance style were built to link the ancient Louvre and Tuileries palaces, and mansarded apartment houses lined the wide boulevards created by Baron Haussmann. Americans and Canadians who visited International Expositions held in the new Paris in 1855 and 1867, even stay-at-homes who saw lithographs and engravings, were captivated. By 1859 architect Samuel Sloan could observe that "the French Roof is in great request. Public and private dwellings and even stables are covered with it, and no man who wants a fashionable house will be without it."

Characteristically, North American Mansard took off in new directions and emerged as a style distinct from its Parisian prototypes and other examples on the Continent. It became popular for major Federal buildings under the auspices of A.B. Mullett, supervising architect of the U.S. Treasury Department, and proved equally adaptable for domestic architecture. Mansard roofs sprang up in villages, towns and suburbs, and the Second Empire style reigned in townhouses from Quebec and Montreal to Philadelphia and even Los Angeles, which consisted mainly of citrus groves until well after the Civil War.

"French roofs" graced public and commercial buildings like the old Clinton Mining Company offices in the booming "silver cities" of Nevada and Colorado and eventually rose along the Main Streets of small towns all over the continent. Since the Second Empire was also called the General Grant style, because of its prevalence during the Civil War and the Union general's subsequent two-term presidency, it is amusing to note that the Grants themselves owned a conventional brick house with white trim (and a flat roof) in Galena, Illinois. However, their interior decor was typically Victorian, complete with heavy carved furniture, gilt mirrors, daguerreotypes, marble mantels, flowered wallpaper and sentimental plaster sculptures by the much-admired John Rogers.

Whether built of cut stone, stucco facing over brick, brownstone, marble, granite, or painted clapboard, the mansard-roofed house provided ample living space for the large Victorian family. It could be modestly trimmed with small brackets below the cornices and an off-center entrance, or lavishly ornamented with stained glass, carving, gingerbread trim, quoins and filigree ironwork. The style had its critics—Lewis Mumford called the mansard roof "a crowning indignity"—but most residents found the Second Empire house dignified, comfortable and commodious, as seen in the plates that follow.

Eastern Style-setters

The immensely popular Italianate style shared many features with the French Second Empire style that became popular during the 1850s. In fact, the cubical villa, with its low-pitched roof replaced by an imposing mansard roof, was readily transformed into a Second Empire house. In the evolutionary way of architecture—an art form available to everyone—mansard roofs and Italianate bracketing were combined in countless ways to create new homes or remodel older ones. Both masonry and wood were employed, with brick and brownstone (weathered sandstone slabs) favored for townhouses. Echoes of earlier styles, both classical and picturesque, were especially resonant on the long-settled East Coast. There, the two highly compatible Italianate and Second Empire styles resulted in some of our most elegant Victorians.

Left: *A mansard-roofed apartment house with Italianate details in Yonkers, New York, one of Westchester County's oldest neighborhoods.*

Above: *Italianate brownstones on New York City's exclusive Gramercy Park, the only remaining private park in the city.*

Right: *Segmental arches—a keynote of the Italianate style—with stone trimwork at the Ammi Whitney House, in Portland, Maine.*

71 ❧

Opposite: *Bracketed porch and roofline detail of the former Jackson's Clubhouse (1872), a gentlemen's gambling house, now the Mainstay Inn in Cape May, New Jersey.*

Above: *An Italianate house with unusual porch, terrace and roofline styling in Ferndale, California.*

Opposite: *The elegant Captain Nathaniel Palmer House, built in Stonington, Connecticut, suggests a colonial clapboard remodeled into an Italianate villa, featuring an octagonal cupola, added for summer ventilation as well as scenic views, bracketed roofline and portico.*

Above: *Designed in 1863 for industrialist George Allen by Samuel Sloan and built by Henri Phillipi in the Bracketed Villa style, the Southern Mansion is a Cape May landmark. Note the square cupola to capture cooling ocean breezes, the double brackets and the tall brick chimney stacks.*

Left: *Bold detailing and a large cupola on a Flemington, New Jersey, villa.*

Opposite: *Paired attic windows with a prominent arch break the cornice line of this Michigan townhouse.*

Below: *A cube-shaped Italianate (1859) in Clinton, New Jersey, a picture-postcard town for lovers of Victoriana.*

Opposite: *French and Italian influences combine in Harrisburg, Pennsylvania's, striking J. Donald Cameron House. Note the hooded dormer windows, second-story oriel on the central tower and intricate stonework.*

Left: *The square Italianate tower, seen here on a home in Morristown, New Jersey, was derived from the campanile, or bell tower, originally built of stone. The famous example at Pisa is unusual in being cylindrical rather than square.*

Above: *A three-story tower breaks the otherwise uniform brick façade of New York's Historical Society of the Tarrytowns's Museum. Located on Grove Street, the museum houses an extensive collection dating back to the 1600s.*

Octagonal Italianates

The Octagon house was promoted vigorously by Orson Squire Fowler, phrenologist and publisher, in his book *A Home for All* (1848). Several thousand examples were built before and after the Civil War, based in part on Fowler's sometimes eccentric ideas about optimum use of space and a healthful environment promoted by air circulation through the rooftop cupola. Many of the octagonal houses were detailed in the Italianate style. Ultimately, the multisided form proved impractical, and the fad had run its course by the late 1860s.

Opposite: *A handsome Octagon villa with Italianate detailing, including the bracketed, finial-topped cupola, in Hudson, Wisconsin.*

Below: *Afternoon winter sunshine lends warmth to this simpler octagonal home in Rhode Island. The unusually large cupola of this Italianate-detailed building houses the flue below a brick chimney.*

François Mansart in North America

Perhaps the most readily identifiable of all the nineteenth-century styles is the French Second Empire, with its distinctive mansard roofline, whether concave, convex, or S-shaped. The Mansard style, as it is often called, dates back to the French Renaissance architect François Mansart (1598–1666), whose influence reigned in the impressive city planning of Paris by Georges Eugène Haussmann during the reign of Napoleon III (1852–70). Several international expositions held in the French capital had a marked effect on American and Canadian architecture from 1855 through the 1870s. In many examples, a dominant square tower was combined with a mansard roof to form a Franco-Tuscan hybrid. The French roof also served to increase usable attic space and provide rich possibilities for ornamentation in the form of iron crestwork, ornate dormer-window moldings and bracketed eaves.

Left: *A fashionable Norwalk, Connecticut, mansion, beautifully restored and landscaped, is now maintained as a commercial property.*

Below: *Beaconsfield, with elegant finial atop a mansard roof in Charlottetown, houses the Prince Edward Island Museum and Heritage Foundation.*

Bottom: *Oakhurst (1874–77), built by the Fulton family in Rockport, Texas, with asymmetrical façade, ornamental quoins and finial-topped tower.*

Above and left: *High-flying mansard rooflines crown fashionable townhouses in Montreal. The example above features decorative ironwork, which was popular in Paris.*

Opposite: *The Ginner-Harter House, a Pittsburgh, Pennsylvania, mansion with a prominent central dormer in the Second Empire style.*

Right: *Roselawn,
an eclectic, lavishly
embellished Queen Anne
Revival house with
mansard-roofed tower
and Eastlake-inspired
gable in Flemington,
New Jersey.*

Below: *Ornate double
brackets figure in both
Italianate and Second
Empire detailing, which
share roots in the
Italian Renaissance as
interpreted in France.*

Bottom: *A crested
campanile and a
mansard roof share
the façade with a
guardian angel over
the doorway of Victoria
Hall in Pittsburgh.*

Eclectic Mediterranean-Influenced Victorian Homes

It was common for houses built in the mid- and late-nineteenth century to blend elements of Italianate and French styles freely, as seen in the melange of details on each of these examples. Many members of the American Institute of Architects, founded in 1857, had trained at the *École des Beaux Arts* and they experimented imaginatively with European forms, especially for wealthy clients. Their ideas were widely adopted, and numerous short-lived fashions found expression in vernacular homes of the period. Shingle, stickwork, Eastlake and appliqué detailing were combined with Italianate shapes and French rooflines, each house becoming a style unto itself.

Opposite: *Late nineteenth-century eclecticism as seen at whaling captain Edward Penniman's house in Eastham, Massachusetts, complete with brackets, quoins, bays and columned entryway.*

Left: *A mansard-roofed Queen Anne with elaborately ornamented dormers in fashionable Summit, New Jersey.*

Below: *The French Empire (with Greek Revival elements on the porch) wins the West in the town of Coupeville, on Washington State's scenic Whidbey Island.*

89 ❧

Opposite: *A narrow San Francisco Italianate with an unusual roofline showing Mansard influence, among others.*

Right: *A San Francisco mansion based on the palazzo model, with a distinctive façade featuring a bay at right and rounded tower at left, and an irregular bracketed roofline.*

Overleaf: *Two Texas-style Mansard façades on San Antonio's King William Street, the state's first area to be designated a historic district.*

Below: *Harmoniously and labor-intensively colored "Eastlake" detailing adorns a colorful townhouse on Oak Street, in San Francisco.*

The Queen Anne Revival

The exuberant style known as the Queen Anne Revival reached North America more than a decade after it became popular in Great Britain. There, it was one of several related styles that emerged in the late 1860s among young architects dissatisfied with strict Gothic Revival forms. For domestic architecture, they looked toward the vernacular in its various modes, and to the "Old English"—Jacobean, Elizabethan and Tudor models. The result was a picturesque, eclectic style rooted in local materials and craftsmanship and respectful of the relationship between house and site. Ornament of various kinds was valued for its own sake, and the emphasis was on comfort and homeliness.

Leaders of the Queen Anne Revival included Philip Webb, Eden Nesfield and Richard Norman Shaw. The movement ranged far more widely than the brief reign of Queen Anne (1702–14), as seen in the English country houses that drew upon centuries of local building tradition, including two of Webb's manor houses: Clouds, in Wiltshire (1879), and Standen, in Sussex (1892). One of his best-known houses is the one designed in 1859 for William Morris—the Red House, in Bexleyheath, Kent. Its simple Gothic-style

Previous pages:
*Both classical
and Gothic elements
articulate the tower
of a Queen Anne in
Summit, New Jersey.*

*An ornate domed roof
crowned by an elaborate
cupola and a tall
patterned chimney
suggest the axiom
"More is more."*

exterior combined circular windows to light the upstairs hall and wooden sash windows crowned by segmental arches. Polychrome slate roofs and elaborate chimney pots emphasized the rambling, asymmetrical form of the house, which looked as if it might have stood for centuries. The interior was richly embellished with stained glass by the gifted painter Edward Burne-Jones, wooden paneling and built-in sideboards and settles in the medieval mode, and elegant wallpaper and painted furniture designed by Morris and his colleagues.

Especially influential in bringing the Queen Anne/Vernacular Revival from England was architect Charles F. Annesley Voysey. His simple country houses included Broadleys on Lake Windermere, Cumbria (1898), with ample bows and broad eaves that overhung bands of second-story casement windows. Norman Shaw's late work was equally influential, including his red brick townhouses with white-trimmed sash windows and gabled dormers. From such attractive prototypes, American and Canadian architects and builders drew inspiration for their own imaginative, colorful and lavishly decorated houses across the continent.

Most Queen Anne Revival houses were built with a large porch—an outdoor sitting room that unites house and grounds, much as sliding doors inside provided an open, flexible ground-floor plan. The porch, or verandah, may encircle two or three sides of the building. Spindle- and spoolwork, pendant gingerbread trim and lacy floral motifs decorate railings, gables, towers and eaves. Incised brackets in the Italianate style, with leaf/flower or geometric detailing, are often painted in a harmonious palette of four to six colors: the overall color scheme of the Queen Anne unites disparate elements into a pleasing whole. Cornice-level moldings, jig-sawn bargeboards, fishscale shingles, fanciful tower roofs and patterned tilework and shingling contribute to the polychrome effect of these elegant "painted ladies." Appliqué work in the form of terra-cotta panels, sunburst motifs, decorative tiles and stone or brick laid in patterned courses were all used to create houses brimming with character and diversity.

As a result of improved technology and transportation, the picturesque Queen Anne Revival spread rapidly during the late nineteenth century to become the reigning style in domestic architecture. Fortunately, notable examples have been preserved across the continent, some as multigenerational family homes, others by clear-sighted local and regional preservation societies. Both towns and cities have refurbished Victorian neighborhoods that had deteriorated into streets full of shabby rowhouses and awkwardly divided rooming houses.

Among the premier examples of this culminating Victorian style are many houses that conform to John Maass's observation in *The Gingerbread Age*: "Victorian buildings are perfect symbols of an era that was not given to understatement. They are in complete harmony with the heavy meals, strong drink, elaborate clothes, ornate furnishings, flamboyant art, melodramatic plays…[and] flowery speeches of the age."

Some of the best-known examples are in San Francisco's Western Addition, Pacific Heights and Dolores Heights, ranging from peak-roofed cottages and townhouses to the sprawling Alfred Clarke House (known as Nobby Clarke's Folly), at the head of Eureka Valley. Designed by Colley and Gould in 1890, it cost a princely sum for the time—$25,000—and commanded a seventeen-acre site.

During the building boom of the late 1880s, the journal *California Architect and Building News* had a great deal to report. Southern California saw its first major expansion, as grand houses and hotels sprang up from Los Angeles to San Diego, site of the Stick-style Del Coronado Hotel (1888). Unfortunately, West Coast building stumbled to a halt during the financial panic of 1894 to 1898. When it recovered at the turn of the century, the Edwardian era was displacing the Victorian.

Farther north, the Canadian city of Victoria, British Columbia, continued to flourish as a result of shipping, lumber and railroad interests, as well as the Klondike gold rush. Eager American travelers embarked upon the *Princess Victoria* and other elegant cruisers operating daily between Seattle, Victoria and Vancouver. Attractions included the lavish Empress Hotel, with its palm-lined, skylit conservatory, and architect Samuel Maclure's imposing Government House. However, Maclure's major work was in residential design for Victoria's leading citizens, including Premier James Dunsmuir's Hatley Park and clothier Biggerstaff Wilson's Elizabethan Revival mansion on Rockland Avenue.

Enterprising late-Victorian entrepreneurs like the Palliser brothers, George and Charles, made their fortunes by selling house plans through the mail. They charged twenty-five cents per copy for their first book, *Model Homes for the People.* When a potential client chose one of the forty-eight models pictured, he or she wrote to describe the site and special requirements and received working drawings at a fraction of the normal cost. One of George Palliser's favorite designs was his own Queen Anne-style house in Bridgeport, Connecticut. It appeared on the cover of his *American Cottage Homes* (1878) and was copied by a Richford, Vermont, merchant named Sheldon Boright, who called the house Grey Gables (1890). A lovely example of the style, this multigabled house has a wraparound porch with turned posts, delicate window surrounds with Adam-style carving, pilasters, cornices and a patterned-shingle roof with iron crestwork. Grey Gables has been restored, like many picturesque Victorians, for use as a bed and breakfast inn.

The South has its share of "gingerbread houses" in the Queen Anne style, which was congenial to outdoor living in a hot climate. One famous example is the Asendorf House (1899), built in Savannah, Georgia, by a member of the German community. He customized a standard boxlike building with extravagant porches and balconies of lathe-turned spindles, balusters and posts arranged around basket arches. Farther west, *nouveau riche* miners, cattlemen, ranchers and financiers commissioned grand (and grandiose) houses that proclaimed their affluence and became landmarks in their communities. They were copied widely on a more modest scale, with decorative touches and materials indigenous to the region.

Not all observers were enamored with the Queen Anne style, which was sometimes described as "Eastlake," for the English architect, artist and furniture designer Charles Locke Eastlake. In his 1872 book *Hints on Household Taste*, he had advocated such interior decorations as panels with carved and incised designs, ornamental moldings and bands of spoolwork spindles. With typical enthusiasm, Americans and Canadians had taken these features outdoors and used them to detail their Queen Anne houses, to the dismay of Eastlake himself. In 1882 he lodged a public protest, declaring: "I now find, to my amazement, that there exists on the other side of the Atlantic an 'Eastlake style' of architecture, which, judging from the specimens I have seen illustrated, may be said to burlesque such doctrines of art as I have ventured to maintain." Architectural historians took due notice and declared the term "Eastlake" a misnomer, but the general public still blithely uses the terms "Queen Anne" and "Eastlake" almost interchangeably.

Opposite: *The historic McKnight House rises to dizzying heights on River Street in Richford, Vermont.*

Below: *The spacious William Broyles House (1873) in Palestine, Texas, with wrap-around porch.*

The Garden Suburb Aesthetic

In England, the late-century Queen Anne Revival was popularized by such architects as Norman Shaw and Philip Webb, as seen in Shaw's Lowther Lodge (1873), Kensington Gore, London. Now the headquarters of the Royal Geographical Society, it enclosed an open courtyard and had an off-center porch and multiple gables ornamented with rubbed and molded brickwork. Eden Nesfield's charming lodge at Kew Garden (1867), London, was well received, and the London suburb of Bedford Park was advertised by Norman Shaw as "the healthiest place in the world," offering "a Garden and a Bath Room with Hot and Cold water to every house." The ideals of health, beauty and comfort were translated into North American English when the Queen Anne style was seen and embraced at the Centennial Exposition of 1876 in Philadelphia. Variant textures, elaborate chimneys, decorative turrets, fanciful woodwork, intricately multicolored paintwork, bays and gables became the order of the day.

99

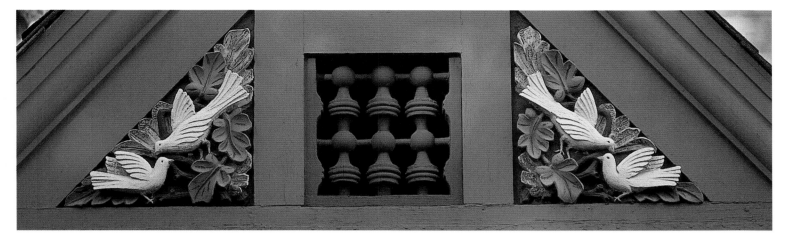

Above: *Birds and botanica found high favor with the romantic Victorians, as seen in this decorative gable detail from the Day House shown at right.*

Right: *The distinctive façade of the Day House in Hartford, Connecticut, combines rusticated stonework and shingled dormers of varied design.*

Opposite: *A serene Canadian Queen Anne in scenic Woodstock, New Brunswick, featuring a wide bay and a spacious porch and terrace.*

Overleaf: *In Rockland, Maine, a beautifully restored house and barn are joined by a breezeway. Both buildings have patterned shinglework, and the gable detailing is reprised in the roof of the barn's cupola.*

101 ❧

Opposite: *Graceful basket arches with turned spoolwork on the porch of a Bay View, Michigan, cottage built in 1875.*

Above: *Romanesque and Palladian arches, cornices, columns and finials adorn the Old Kenrad House (1895) in Gonzales, Texas.*

Right: *A flat cut-out balustrade with a stylized tulip design is typical of the Swiss Chalet mode of decoration.*

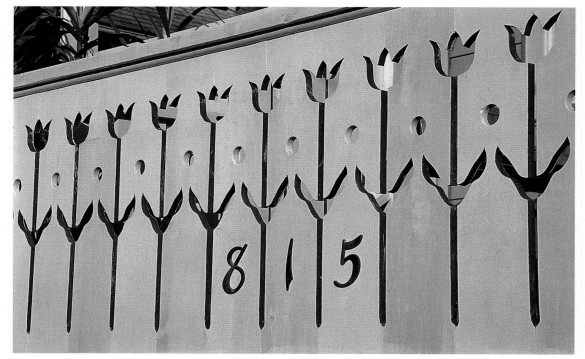

Above: *Exuberant foliage reliefs and twin sunbursts in what is commonly called the Eastlake style, San Francisco.*

Opposite, top: *A roomy turn-of-the-century Queen Anne in coastal Westport, Connecticut, with steeply pointed gable.*

Right: *The gracious, rambling Williams House on Mackinac Island, Michigan, a scenic crossroads on the Great Lakes.*

Townhouse Styles

Several American cities were expanding when the Queen Anne Revival was at its height, including San Francisco, whose Victorian houses and neighborhoods are a national treasure. After the Gold Rush of 1849, a coherent grid plan was devised for the hilly site. Native redwood was the main building material, often milled and painted to resemble stone. A guide to the city published in 1888 pointed out that "The superior facility for shaping wood, and the abundance of machinery for planing and molding, has led to the adoption of more architectural ornament here than in any other city." Built mainly on steep, narrow lots, with elegant façades painted in light-reflecting colors, San Francisco's "painted ladies" have set the standard for Victorian restorations nationwide. Other North American cities with notable Queen Anne townhouses include Pittsburgh and Philadelphia, Pennsylvania; New Albany, Indiana; Saratoga Springs, New York; Savannah, Georgia; and Victoria, British Columbia.

Above: *Terraced rooflines, varied window treatments and gingerbread lace on San Francisco's Alamo Square.*

Left: *Intricate gable and second-story appliqué work in the Bay City drew admiring looks from Eastern vistors.*

Right: *Detail of the geometrically patterned gable of the house at far right, above.*

Opposite: *Detail of the Haas-Lilienthal House, constructed in 1886 for William Haas and now the headquarters of the San Francisco Architectural Heritage Foundation.*

Above: *An ornate straight-sided bay window flanks a decorative entry in Eureka, California.*

Right: *A slant-sided bay with intricate pilasters, dentils, spoolwork and stained-glass panes outlining lower windows at Eureka's historic "Pink Lady."*

Above: *Maximum living space is packed into these narrow, colorful Queen Annes in Reading, Pennsylvania.*

Left: *San Francisco's Steiner Street is a microcosm of the individual effects achieved by the city's late-century Victorians.*

113 ❧

Left: *A shaded street in Cape May, where decorative sleeping porches allow continuous enjoyment of the sea air.*

Opposite: *An inviting Cape May Queen Anne, with multitextured, ornate detailing and a rooftop acroterion.*

Below: *At Ocean Grove Camp Meeting Grounds, pretty summer cottages soon replaced the original tents.*

Overleaf: *Tranquillity reigns at a rambling summer retreat on picturesque Prince Edward Island.*

Summer Places

Some of our most delightful Victorians are found in summer resorts along the New Jersey Shore, coastal Massachusetts and the scenic Great Lakes. Many of these enclaves were founded by religious organizations, including Ocean Grove, New Jersey, which the Camp Meeting Association advertised as "God's Square Mile of Health and Happiness." Middle-class families could enjoy affordable vacations at these various resorts, in cottages ranging from Seaside Chalet, Shingle and Stick styles to purely idiosyncratic. Most had sleeping porches for maximum benefit from the healthful country air. The colorful results are seen from Cape May, New Jersey, and Chatauqua, New York, to Bay View, Michigan.

Below: *A spoolwork sunburst crowns an elegant gable window with geometric leading.*

Bottom: *An intricately painted detail of the famous J.M. Carson mansion in Eureka.*

Right: *Gilded and painted details on an arched façade with radiating grillework.*

Experiments in Opulence

Between the Civil War and 1900, the United States experienced rampant economic growth, except in the Deep South, which was quite slow to recover from the ravages of war on its own soil. Elsewhere, some amazing experiments in domestic architecture embodied the eclectic, sometimes excessive, styles of the century. Many proved impractical—or impossible—to keep up, and were demolished, or converted into museums of Victoriana. Others have been refurbished and modified for twentieth-century life, sounding a colorful note that affirms the presence of the past in our communities.

Opposite: A boldly recolored Queen Anne cottage designed by the Newsom Brothers (1893) in Eureka, California, site of the grandiose Carson Mansion (detail shown on page 118).

Below: Detail of the radiating spindlework framing the horseshoe-arched portico of the cottage on the opposite page.

Above: *The Gingerbread Mansion in Ferndale, California, exemplifies the lavish ornamentation and coloring used more often on West Coast houses than on their East Coast counterparts.*

Below: *An eclectic Victorian on San Francisco's Steiner Street (porch detail shown on page 119) leaves no decorative stone unturned, from curving balustrades to lacy rooftop acroteria.*

Opposite: *The Armour-Stiner House in Westchester County, New York, one of only two Romantic Octagons in the country. The eclectic dome was added by the second owner, Joseph Stiner, in 1872.*

Victorian Interiors

The stiffly posed formal photographs of Victorian families against somber-looking backgrounds bear little resemblance to the people shown or the homes in which they lived. What was then the new art of studio photography required long, immobile exposures and serious expressions. Smiling for the camera was actively discouraged, and artificial backdrops contributed to the impression of unease. Thanks to Mathew Brady's imposing portraits and countless family albums, later generations saw their nineteenth-century forebears as rigid, solemn and constrained in demeanor, which is far from the truth. The spirit of the age is reflected in the beauty, diversity and, often, playfulness of Victorian homes, which were not only shrines to domesticity, but expressions of the wide-ranging interests, energies, culture and tastes of the era. Victorian decor offers fascinating glimpses of the inner lives of the enterprising men and women who claimed more than half a continent in less than half a century.

The Victorian house, whether new or remodeled, contained both formal and informal rooms. The front parlor and dining room were usually the "best-dressed," while

Previous pages:
The impressive grand staircase of Fair Lane, the estate of Henry and Clara Bryant Ford (exterior picture on pages 32–33), with rich wood paneling, intricate banister rail carving and stained glass.

Decorative plaster molding detail from the Molly Stark House, in Dunbarton, New Hampshire.

the back parlor and bedrooms were more informal. In the typical multistoried house, the utility areas were grouped on connecting levels, from the basement laundry room to the servant's room, or rooms, above the kitchen and pantry. This region of the house had its own staircase, removed from the main staircase that usually ascended from the entrance hall.

On narrow city lots, townhouses of various styles made economical use of space by building in line, from the bay-windowed front parlor to the back parlor, dining room and kitchen. On the second floor, the master bedroom usually faced the street, and smaller children's bedrooms succeeded it, followed by the servant's quarters. In three-story houses, most domestics were housed in the attic. By the latter part of the nineteenth century, such former luxuries as indoor bathrooms with running water were being taken for granted as more and more houses were equipped with electric or gas lighting, telephones and central heating.

Landscaping and gardening, even on a small scale, were vital to house-proud Victorian families. Local journalists spoke in glowing terms of the attractive grounds that enhanced their communities, and house-plan books showed settings for their "Venetian Summer Residences" and "Gothic Cottages." The passion for order and progress was reflected in the garden suburb, where a bewildering variety of styles coexisted peacefully on the same tree-shaded block. As architect Gervase Wheeler pointed out in his widely read pattern book *Sketches of Houses Suited to American Country Living*: "An architect who has the interests of his noble science at heart will *always* insist on studying the site and the tastes of habits of life of the future occupants." Budget permitting, a landscape architect was often retained to design picturesque pathways and pergolas that opened onto lacy gazebos, formal flower beds, statuary in niches, graceful benches framed by climbing roses, even lawn tennis courts and ornamental ponds.

The love of flowers and exotic plants was reflected indoors in the profusion of floral wallpapers, textiles and paintings. Botanical motifs were carved in wood and carried out in plaster moldings, ceiling rosettes, ornate capitals and corbels. Conservatories were in great demand, and potted palms and ferns were ubiquitous.

The entryway was enhanced by patterned marble floor tiles and mosaics of classical and Oriental inspiration. Often, front doors were paired and varnished to display their paneled woodwork; elegant bronze and wrought-iron hardware lent solidity. Metal crestwork and fencing created patterns of light and shadow, reprised by interior spindlework, balustrades and openwork screens.

Critics have often characterized Victorian furniture as heavy and uncomfortable. However, the plates that follow illustrate the colorful richness and diversity of period furniture. Popular designers included England's Charles Locke Eastlake, who espoused the revival of Gothic and Jacobean styles; the Thomas Chippendales, father and son, masters of the Rococo, who borrowed freely from French and Chinese designs; and Michael Thonet, whose Austrian factories produced the famous bentwood furniture of the day. He developed the process of bending wood under steam heat to produce profusely curved ornamental furniture. Domestic cabinetmakers and designers produced curvilinear, deeply upholstered sofas and chairs, dining-room suites, bedsteads and bureaus in native woods like oak, cherry, pine and walnut, as well as imported teak and mahogany. In 1876 the Philadelphia firm of Gould & Company offered a "Solid Walnut Italian Marble-top Chamber [bedroom] Suite" of nine pieces for $55.00.

The passion for collecting curious and exotic items from seashells and beadwork to china and plaster statuary had its effect on furniture design in the form of multitiered mantels and shelving on which to display these treasures. Bowfront cabinets with etched-glass doors, and built-in carved sideboards served the same purpose. Fringed cushions, ottomans, family photographs, needlepoint samplers, doilies, antimacassars and wax flowers under glass domes vied for space on every surface. Le Corbusier's dictum "Less is more" would have drawn a blank stare from Victorian decorators.

Window treatments included blinds and shutters for privacy and a wide range of muslin and lace curtains, with or without velvet drapery and tasseled valances. Handsome parquet floors of various patterns and lavish floral carpets—sometimes replicated on a painted ceiling—were the height of fashion. Carved wainscoting, elaborate newel posts and ornamental hat racks and umbrella stands abounded.

As wealth and family size grew, existing houses were often remodeled with artwork and furnishings acquired abroad by second- and third-generation Americans and Canadians whose grandfathers had made their marks on the New World. Exotic Revival embellishments included Moorish-style arches, tilework with beautiful Arabic calligraphy, minarets and subtle stone colors contrasted with brilliant decorative details. All of these elements appear in the Moorish-style villa designed by landscape painter Frederic Edwin Church for a site overlooking the Hudson River, in Hudson, New York. Captivated by a two-year tour of the Middle East, Church spent years building his dream house, Olana, with architect Calvert Vaux. Church chose and mixed the colors for every room and designed the exterior and interior stencils in a style he called "Personal Persian."

The mansions that were commissioned by the continent's wealthiest families, including the famous Four Hundred of New York City society, far exceeded all previous definitions of opulence. Their massive French Renaissance and Italianate townhouses include many National Landmarks, as do the Newport "cottages" of the Gilded Age. As the Rhode Island city became an increasingly desirable resort, its premier location, Ochre Point, was crowned with a series of magnificent estates. They included Alva Smith Vanderbilt's Marble House (1892) and Cornelius Vanderbilt II's country house, The Breakers (1895), both designed by Richard Morris Hunt.

One hundred craftsmen were brought from Italy to cut and polish the blocks of gleaming marble—Carrara, Siena, Algerian and more—that comprised the halls of Alva Vanderbilt's monument. Entire rooms were fabricated in France, disassembled and shipped to Newport for installation. They included the Versailles-inspired Gold Room that served as a ballroom and the baronial hall that housed the owner's collection of Gothic art. Not to be outdone by her sister-in-law, Alice Vanderbilt, the wife of Cornelius II, was instrumental in "Corneil's" expenditure of $7 million for The Breakers, exclusive of furnishings imported from Europe. The grandiose Italian Renaissance-style mansion, clad in Indiana limestone, rose four stories and contained some seventy rooms and thirty bathrooms. Its great central hall was designed with a vaulted ceiling forty-five feet high, filled with polychromed stenciling, and a pavement composed of colored marble. As the twentieth century dawned, Victorian America and Canada could—and did—survey their achievements with complacency, and with the firm expectation of still greater things to come.

Right: *Wallpaper of Chinese inspiration, a handsome marble fireplace and graceful chandelier in the dining room of the Rotch-Jones-Duff House, New Bedford, Massachusetts.*

Opposite: *An elegant classical dining room at the Henry Ford mansion, Fair Lane, connected to the parlor by sliding "pocket doors." In keeping with European aristocratic homes, ancestral portraits adorn the dining room walls.*

Stately Dining Rooms

Grand settings for formal dining were a hallmark of the Victorian age. Appearances—of wealth and social status—were considered far more important than practicalities, and servants often had to carry laden platters from the far side of the house, or even another story, for well-to-do families and their guests.

Stained and Leaded Glass

Decorative multicolored and -paned windows were essential to Gothic decor, forming patterns of light and color in stairwells, foyers, parlors, master bedrooms and libraries.

Left: *Detail of a triple window designed by J.B. Tiffany at Wilderstein, in Rhinebeck, New York.*

Below: *A medieval-style "picture window" at the imposing Turnblad mansion in Minneapolis, Minnesota.*

Opposite: *The Gothic study and mullioned cathedral window at Woodstock, Connecticut's, Roseland Cottage, built in 1846 for Henry Chandler Bowen. Maintained by the Society for the Preservation of New England Antiquities, the house contains many of its original furnishings.*

Carved and Paneled Woodwork

Ornately sculpted decorative trim and heavy, rich wood paneling embellished many a lavish estate built in the halcyon days of fortunes made at the turn of the twentieth century.

Above and opposite: *Midwestern mansions enriched by intricate detailing drawn from nature and from classical prototypes.*

Right: *Wall detail of the oak-paneled library at Wilderstein, added to the original house built by Thomas Suckley in 1852 by Arnout Cannon, Jr., in 1888.*

Grand Staircases

Rising from the formal entrance and foyer, wide, sweeping staircases, often with elaborately carved woodwork and stained-glass picture windows at the landings, were added to create a baronial impression of vistas unfolding in new splendor on the upper levels.

Right: *A monumental effect achieved by stonework, asymmetrical massing and multilevel balustrades.*

Opposite: *Chandeliers and torchières light the way to the Gothic-style gallery above at Meadow Brook Hall, the Dodge House, outside Detroit.*

Bedchambers and Dressing Rooms

The bedroom, called "the chamber" and considered a feminine domain and a private retreat, was usually less formal than the common rooms downstairs. Soothing colors often prevailed, and furnishings included washstands and urns when plumbing was not connected to the upper stories.

Opposite: *A sunny bedroom at Charlottetown's Beaconsfield, with a marble-topped vanity, gracefully upholstered chair and carved blanket chest.*

Below: *An artless children's room, depicted as "Anne's Room" at the Green Gables House in Prince Edward Island National Park.*

Below: *An antique doll in period dress presides over a miniature chinaware tea set at carefully preserved Beaconsfield, a Victorian-era mansion designed by W.C. Harris in Charlottetown, Prince Edward Island.*

Right: *A child's bedroom preserved at the White Dove Cottage in Cape May, New Jersey, a National Historic community.*

Left: *Moses Eaton stenciling in the central hallway of the Molly Stark House, Dunbarton, New Hampshire.*

Porches and Conservatories

In most regions, shaded outdoor space was essential for the summer months before the advent of air conditioning. Porches and verandahs were widely built across the continent on grand and modest homes alike. In cooler climates, glazed conservatories afforded light and comfort and the opportunity to extend the briefer outdoor season.

Right: *A spacious verandah with ample room for dining and relaxing overlooks a beautiful view in British Columbia.*

Opposite: *Winter vanishes beyond the windows of this lush conservatory, double-glazed and centrally heated during renovations, and furnished with a filigreed Victorian-style conservatory suite.*

Glossary of Architectural Terms

acroterion A pedestal for a sculpture or ornament at the base or apex of a pediment.

architrave The lowermost part of an entablature, resting directly on top of a column in classical architecture.

ashlar The square-edged hewn stones for wall construction laid in horizontal courses with vertical joints.

balustrade A row of miniature columns (balusters) supporting a handrail, used decoratively to frame porches and crown rooftops.

batten A narrow strip of wood used for flooring and siding in alternation with wider boards (called board-and-batten).

bargeboard The projecting boards placed against the gable ends of a house and usually decorated, as in the Victorian mode.

belt course A change of exterior masonry or patterning used to articulate the stories of a building; also called stringcourse.

capital The top part of a column, usually decorated, and larger than the column shaft.

casement window A narrow window with sashes that open outward on hinges.

Castellated A substyle of the Gothic Revival, with notched rooflines called **crenellation**.

cladding A finishing material, like boards or shingles, overlaid on an unfinished wall or roof, whether of timber framing, masonry, or other material.

clapboard A thin board laid horizontally and overlapped to create a weathertight surface on a wooden building.

colonnade A row of columns, often featuring horizontal entablature.

corbel A masonry block projecting from a wall to support a horizontal feature.

cornice A projecting, usually decorative, feature at the top of walls, arches and eaves.

crenellation A pattern of square indentations of medieval inspiration, also called battlements.

dentil One of a series of small rectangular blocks forming a molding, or projecting beneath a cornice.

dormer A vertically positioned window set into, and projecting from, a sloping roof.

eaves The lower edge or edges of a roof that project beyond the wall below.

entablature The horizontal upper section of a classical order, resting on the capital and including the architrave, frieze and cornice.

fanlight A semicircular window, often with sash bars arranged like the ribs of a fan.

fenestration The arrangement of the windows and/or doors of a house.

finial A vertical ornament fixed to the peak of a roof or tower, used especially in Gothic styles.

fretwork An ornamental feature consisting of three-dimensional geometric designs or other symmetrical figures (frets) enclosed in a band or border.

friezeboard A decorative band around a wall.

gable A triangular wall area enclosed by the rising edges of a sloping roof.

gambrel roof A ridged roof with two slopes on each side, the lower slope having the steeper pitch. Often used on barns and neo-Dutch colonial buildings.

half-timbering A type of timber-frame construction in which the surfaces between posts and beams are filled in with another material, like stucco or brick, leaving part of the timber framing exposed.

hip roof One on which the external angle is formed by the meeting of two adjacent sloping sides.

hood molding An ornamental surround framing the upper part of a window.

lintel A horizontal beam or stone placed over door or window openings.

loggia An arcaded or roofed gallery projecting from the side of a house and often overlooking an open court.

mansard roof One with a double slope on all four sides, the lower slope being steeper than the upper.

modillion A rectangular bracket supporting a cornice that indicates an extension of rafters through the wall.

mullion A slender vertical bar used in dividing the panes of a window.

oculus window A circular window in the upper story or the dome of a building.

ogee arch An arch of two curves meeting at a point, as in Oriental architecture; also, a double curve with the shape of an elongated "S."

oriel window The upper-story bay window supported by a corbel or bracket.

parquet floor A floor covering of hardwood blocks laid in geometric patterns.

pediment A low triangular element, framed by horizontal sloping cornices, usually found at the gable ends of a Greek temple between the frieze and the roof; most often used in residential architecture as a decorative element over doorways.

pendant A gable ornament suspended from the peak and often flanked by **bargeboards**.

pier A supporting post, usually square, shorter and thicker than a column.

pilaster A shallow support or pier attached to a wall, usually rectangular, used especially for decoration of doorways and fireplaces.

portico A colonnaded entry porch.

quatrefoil An ornament composed of four clover-like lobes radiating from a common center and offset by triangular cusps between each lobe.

quoin A rectangle of stone or brick used in a vertical series to decorate the corners of a building and façade openings.

sash The framework or mullion that holds the glass panes in a window.

sidelights The narrow windows flanking a doorway.

siding The boards, shingles, or other material used to surface a frame building.

stepped gable One constructed with a series of steps or curves along the roof slope, but independent of it. Often seen in Flemish and German architecture.

stickwork The exterior patterned woodwork that serves an ornamental rather than a structural purpose.

stringcourse *see* **beltcourse**

stucco A durable finish for exterior walls, usually composed of cement, sand and lime.

trefoil A three-lobed ornament used in Gothic Revival styles, often in the form of a window.

valence Fabric arranged in vertical folds hung from a cornice above a window.

vault An arched roof or ceiling, as in a rotunda.

wainscoting The woodwork that panels the lower portion of a room.

witch's cap A shingled, conical tower roof.

Index

Page numbers in **boldface** refer to illustrations.

Bibliography

Clark, Clifford Edward, Jr. *The American Family Home: 1800–1960*. Chapel Hill: Univ. of North Carolina Press, 1986.

Delehanty, Randolph, and Richard Sexton. *In the Victorian Style*. S.F.: Chronicle Books, 1991.

Dixon, Roger, and Stefan Muthesius. *Victorian Architecture*, World of Art series. London: Thames and Hudson, 1978.

Foreman, John, and Robbe Pierce Stimson. *The Vanderbilts and the Gilded Age: Architectural Aspirations, 1879–1901*. N.Y.: St. Martin's Press, 1991.

Gill, Brendan, and Dudley Witney. *Summer Places*. N.Y.: Methuen, 1978.

Guild, Robin. *The Victorian House Book*. N.Y.: Rizzoli, 1989.

Kouwenhoven, John A. *The Columbia Historical Portrait of New York: An Essay in Graphic History*. N.Y.: Harper & Row, 1972.

Maass, John. *The Gingerbread Age: A View of Victorian America*. N.Y.: Rinehart & Co., 1957

Naversen, Kenneth. *East Coast Victorians: Castles & Cottages*. Wilsonville, Oregon: Beautiful America Publishing, 1990.

Pomada, Elizabeth, and Michael Larsen. *America's Painted Ladies: The Ultimate Celebration of Our Victorians*. N.Y.: Penguin Books USA, 1992.

Scully, Vincent. *The Architecture of the American Summer: The Flowering of the Shingle Style*, Documents of American Architecture series. N.Y.: Rizzoli, 1989.

Walker, Lester. *American Shelter: An Illustrated Encyclopedia of the American Home*. Woodstock, N.Y.: Overlook Press, 1981.

Zingman-Leith, Elan and Susan, with Tim Fields. *The Secret Life of Victorian Houses*. Wash., D.C.: Elliott & Clark, 1993.

Zukowsky, John, and Robbe Pierce Stimson. *Hudson River Villas*. N.Y.: Rizzoli, 1985.

Acknowledgements

The publisher would like to thank the following individuals for their assistance in the preparation of this book: Nicola J. Gillies, editor; Charles J. Ziga, art director and photographer; Wendy Ciaccia Eurell, graphic designer; Jay Olstad for supplementary research and photography; and Annie Lise Roberts for her architecture expertise. Grateful acknowledgement is also made to the communities of the featured houses, travel and tourism agencies, historical societies across the continent and the photographers and agencies listed below for permission to reproduce the photographs on the following pages: © **Kindra Clineff 1999**: 8, 19, 36–37b, 45b, 80, 125, 129, 139b; © **Robert Drapala**: 51b, 114b; © **Rudi Holnsteiner**: 4, 18, 53, 83b, 99, 104t; © **Balthazar Korab**: 10, 13, 20, 21, 30–31 (both), 32–33, 36t, 39, 55t, 60, 61, 62–63 (both), 64–65 (both), 76, 81, 92, 93, 105, 107b, 124, 128, 130b, 132, 133t, 134, 135, 140, 141; © **Jay Olstad**: 1, 9, 12, 24, 130t (permission of Wilderstein Preservation, Rhinebeck, New York), 133b (permission of Wilderstein Preservation, Rhinebeck, New York); © **John Sylvester**: 43, 47b, 83t, 100, 116–17, 136, 137, 138; © **Charles J. Ziga**: 2, 6, 7, 11, 15, 22–23, 25 (both), 26–27 (both), 28 (both), 29 (both), 34 (both), 35, 38, 42, 44, 45t, 46, 47t, 48 (both), 49, 50–51t, 52, 54, 55b, 56–57 (both), 58–59 (both), 66, 67, 70–71 (all), 72, 73, 74, 75, 77 (both), 78, 79 (both), 82, 84 (both), 85, 86–87 (all), 88, 89 (both), 90, 91 (both), 94, 95, 101 (both), 102–103, 104b, 106, 107t, 108–109 (all), 110 (both), 111, 112–13 (both), 114t, 115, 118–19 (all), 120 (both), 121, 122, 123; **Chamber of Commerce of Greater Cape May**: 139t; **Charleston Area Convention & Visitors Bureau**: 14; **Courtesy of the Society for the Preservation of New England Antiquities**: 131 (© David Bohl); **Vermont Department of Tourism & Marketing**: 98.